je suis noir | i am black

selected poems

by

C. Lilley

Table of Contents

Foreword

"Je suis noir."
"I am black."

This phrase has for centuries been regarded as one of the most resolute declarations and one of the most taboo utterances... No matter what language it is spoken in.

Too often ink and breath has been hushed at the mere mention of this phrase. Whether by media, or politics, or vigilantes, or law enforcement, the very idea of blackness has been swept under rugs, locked behind bars, and laid to rest in cemeteries across this country and across the world.

While calls for unity concerning other important world topics have been largely met with minimal opposition, the cries to address the injustices done to black people right here in America have gone largely ignored. We've been asked to ignore a history that still impacts us to this day in pursuit of "progress".

As a black man, I've watched news stories within the past five years littered with the injustices done to my people...with the bodies of my people. I've seen black lives demonized by media and claimed by undeserving gun metal and extrajudicial whim. I've seen the phrase "Black Lives Matter" create visceral reactions within citizens of America, who are determined to tell us our struggle is not unique. I've seen those who try to convince themselves that we now live in a post-racial America and that they no longer see race attempt to erase our Black history with their blindness. I've seen white people don black face at both Halloween parties and in NAACP board meetings without having to worry about the discrimination and hatred often associated with this skin. I've seen hoodies, and skittles, and Arizona, and stolen cigarettes, and toy guns, and running, and resistance, and breathing, and living… be condemnable by death. I will not ignore our history. I will no longer be silent.

This book serves to give the black voice wings. To give perspective into the black experience that has long since been defined for us. To allow black life the rare opportunity to be expressed in an unblemished and unbiased way… to operate outside of the realm of politics, or stereotype, or law, or popular media and to just be expressed, unapologetically. To give a resting place to the souls lost simply because of the color of their skin. To give those lives slain their proper level of sadness, mourning, and anger, and to give their names proper recognition and humanity. To show that this is not just a black issue, but an issue that affects us all, and that the best way to help is to first understand our hearts. To give this issue the brain space it is so often denied and to open up the conversation about what can be done to stop the injustices done to my people. To our people.

"Je suis noir. Nous sommes noirs."
"I am black. We are black."

-Damone Johnson

Preface

In the year 2015, the city of Paris was rocked by two separate terror attacks; one in January and one in November. The world was quick to stand in solidarity with France in the wake of these two tragedies. All over social media, there were different hashtags that grew in popularity (*je suis Charlie, je suis francais, prayers for France, etc.*) as a result of the overwhelming support the Western world showed those who would have the nerve to attack such a beautiful city.

I stood in support of Paris. I tweeted the hashtag, I reposted the flag, and I prayed the prayers. However, there was something disconcerting about the whole situation. In the midst of the attacks, there was no question. France needs our support. But there was always a question when a person of colour would fall to police brutality and violence. Don't get me wrong. Some of those who were in the process of being arrested deserved just that; an arrest. No more, no less. Instead, black blood was shed and black lives were lost. And while there were some who were quick to join the cry that black lives matter, it wasn't nearly as unanimous as *je suis francais.*

This is not to diminish the tragedies in France. Both attacks were heinous crimes against humanity. Period. Full stop.

But I also want to recognize the great tragedy that is the loss of black lives in America and the resulting debate about whether or not people of colour matter. This chapbook is a direct response to these feelings. Saying black lives matter is not to say ONLY black lives matter or ONLY black tragedies matter. But rather, it is a response to a culture that diminishes the attacks on people of colour, discredits their innocence, and disparages our race as a whole. *je suis noir* is a work that stands in support of Black communities suffering the effects of racial violence.

je suis noir is not meant to minimize French tragedies. *je suis noir* is a cry that says "our tragedies are valid as well."

My name is Christopher Shawn-Michael Lilley. I am a Christian, a singer, a songwrite, a teacher, a son, an older brother, a husband.. I am also a black poet who will not remain silent while this nation murders black people. I have a right to be angry.

-C. Lilley

I dedicate this
To little black boys and girls
Who were told they can't

Hemiola

Deep in my heart
There is a fusion
Of Djembe and Violin
Of Siyahamba and Partita
Of Tshotsholoza and Sinfonia
Of Drum Circle and Orchestra
The meeting of two worlds
Melding tribes and empires
Making musical masterpiece of opposite coasts
Making heartbeat out of hemiola

Untitled

(After 'Song' by Gwendolyn Bennett)

This be the culmination of dichotomy
Of black-toned skin and pale-coloured history
Of royalty and poverty
This be the fusion of
Fiction and fact of
Tears and triumphs
This be the juxtaposition
Of vocabulary and urban dictionary
Of spiritual and aria

This is my song
A song of contradiction
A song of contrast
Housing fear and pride
Modern holocaust and Pentecost
Heritage and self-genocide
Preservation and gentrification
And it's hard, you know.
Being one man with many faces
Being class clown and town cryer in the same
breath
Being one with a grieving mother
Being professional hoodlum
Being educated malcontent

Being white-washed blackface.

Ode to the Dark Boy

Young dark boy
Preacher of the pretty boy swag
Prophet of Pac and Biggie
K-Dot and J. Cole
Missionary of the hi-top fade
The dreadlock
The black fist afro pick
Minister of the Harlem Shake
The Dougie and the Whip
Cabbage Patch and Humpty Dance
You are divine
A son of God
A prince.
Your hands and feet
And all that lie in between
Are regal
Meant to tread on rose petals
Ruler of all you survey
You are builder
You are grower
You are pastor
You are activist
You are dreamer
You are precious
You are black diamond
You are lion
You are man

Myth
Legend
You are legendary.

Ode to the Dark Girl

Young dark girl
Empress
Queen
Evangelist of the hot comb
The curling iron
The corn row
The box braid
Emissary of the Carefree Black Girl Gospel
Amen
Amen to your strength
Amen to your fragrance
Amen to your hands
Those instruments of wonder
Creating masterpieces
At home
The workplace
The battlefield
Amen to your black girl magic
How you are so much more
Than curves and chocolate
Your very skin is fertile ground
For your grandest dreams
Dream on, Dark girl
Dark queen
Dark empress
Amen.

Another Man's Treasure

I do not:

Hate you
Wish upon you the fates of my brethren.
Pray for the extinguishing of your breath.
Prey on the skulls of your children.
Find pleasure in your pain.
Equate your existence to the River Styx.
Expect your body to be street silhouette.
Call your body empty, a forfeit container.
Think that your life is a fire sale.
Hold disdain for your worth.
Count you as object, an ordinary dead thing

You are not:
Fetish.
Target.
Punchline.
Casket
Pet
Problem
Animal
Slave

You are a cryptic being
All mysticism and mystery
And worthy of love.

Loving you shall be a game
Played with warm hands
And open fingers.
And your memory shall be
As sunrise and sunset
As tides wax and wane
As seasons change.
Always quiet
Always beautiful.

This Time
(After Charleston)

i.

'Oh deep in my heart
I do believe
We shall overcome someday'

I'm tired of singing this song.
I'm tired of writing this poem.
I'm tired of building cemeteries and memorials out
of my words.
I'm tired and there doesn't seem to be any rest in
sight.
This time it was a church.
A prayer meeting.
A collection of those merely seeking God for help
with the bills
Or unruly children
Or depression
Or other things that I don't understand
They say that when praises go up
Blessings come down,
But when their prayers went up
Bullets rained down
As if the answer to each prayer
Was a hole in the chest

Ash

Loving a black man in America be no easy thing
When life is a seed
(with all the potential in the world)
In California Wildfire
Even the tallest sequoia
Strong and stately
Enduring
Nearly everlasting
Can crumble
Dissolve into smoke
In response to
The smallest spark

Film Noir

Mama always said that the movies wasn't real
That those was actors pretending to be happy
Pretending to be angry
She told me that the bad guys always lost
And the good guys always won
Because they were good guys
And God don't let the bad guys win

Mama always said that you can't fight violence with
violence
That the fights in the movies was just dancing
And the blood was just red kool-aid
She told me that the good guys were just better
dancers
And the bad guys ain't have no rhythm
Cuz they ain't grow up with no good music
Like gospel or R&B or Soul

Mama always said that you can't believe everything
you see
Especially if it's on TV
There are lots of people who pretend.
Pretending to be happy
Pretending to be angry
Pretending to hate people
Just cuz they look different

Mama always said that I was a good actor
That I could fake tears better than Hollywood stars
But my fake tears weren't realer than hers
The tears she think I don't see her wipe away
When I gotta come home late from school
Or if she don't know where I'm at
I think mama's a good actor too

Mama always said that I could be anything that I
wanna be
And I think I wanna be an actor.
I wanna pretend to be brave
I wanna pretend to be safe
I wanna pretend to be the good guy
I wanna pretend to be all these things
Cuz ain't no one believe I could be them anyway.

Fairy Tale

If her name had been anything else
It would have been Goldilocks
Hair, waterfalling onto her shoulders
Pools of shimmering brass
Shining suns
Eyes, blue as the skies
And bright and curious
Hands, pale and open
With an insatiable hunger to touch that which
doesn't belong to her
And she grabs
With no regard for history
Or dignity
She replaces her own parts for others
Or rather
She borrows them
Steals them
Claims them as birthright
As Jacob to Esau
Gathers hands with cotton plants for fingers
Gathers skin with broken ground for melanin
Says that these are just right
Says the heritage naturally given here was too cold
Says that history sewn to her skin is too hot

This Time
(After Rachel)

ii.
I'm tired of singing this song.
Of writing this poem.
Of chanting this slogan.
I'm tired of wondering which article of clothing or
item in my pocket
Is an IED
Biding its time
Till another ordinary looking object
Turns into ordinance
Explodes into my body

For far too long
I've seen what discrepancies skin colour can cause.
I've seen men fall because of melanin
And women claim that melanin as their own.
This time it was a white woman.
Acting as if a heritage of darkened skin and slave
ship was something to be acquired
That a timeline of terror fueled nights
Fearing hoses and dogs
Was something you could merely put on as make
up.
I wonder what would happen
if Emmett whistled at Rachel.

Asthma Attack

Can't you?
Can you see?
Can you breathe?
Can you fall and
Gasp?
Don't fight.
Don't gasp and fall.
You can breathe.
You can see.
You can.
…You can't?

Breathe From Hearts

I can't see
I can't breathe
Breathe the air
Breathe the poison
Poison the past
Poison the future
Future children
Future funerals
Funerals are few
Funerals are many
Many are full
Many are empty
Empty chalk outlines
Empty apologies
Apologies for anger
Apologies for mistakes
Mistakes were made
Mistakes weren't made
Made in America
Made from history
History repeats itself till
His story repeats itself
till
Till's story repeats itself
Till's body feeds the
land
Land of the "me"
Land of the free

Free from shackles
Free from chains
Chains yet exist
Chains yet rattle
Rattling breath
Rattling lungs
Lungs can't breathe
Lungs can't plead
Plead for air
Plead for life
Life was simple
Life was sacred
Sacred for them
Sacred for us?
Us against them
Us against the world
World of anger
World broken
Broken bones
Broken Hearts
Hearts of pain
Hearts of darkness.
Pain....
Darkness

To Emmitt

It has been 74 years since your eyes cracked open
Bright and Hazel
Filled with promise
Three quarters of a century
Since your bronzed skin
Felt the bite of a Chicago winter
I want to tell you that we got better
That we learned
That your shoulders
Though they be cotton gin dead weight
That your body
Disfigured and deformed
Soaked in Tallahatchie brine
That your face
Emblazoned across Jet Magazine
Open Casket Holocaust
That your eyes and skin
Hazel and Bronze
Shades of Black is Beautiful
That all of these crushed parts of you
Became revered history
A section in a schoolbook
Never to be repeated
I want to tell you that your story is not current
events
That you are not a predecessor
To a timeline of death

Continuing ad infinitum
I want to tell you
That there is a world
Where your death
Is not replayed
In live-action.

To Mike

I don't know your whole story
I don't know if your hands,
Filled with the potential of a fledgling universe,
Were guilty or innocent
I wasn't there.
I wasn't there when you ran
I wasn't there when you raised your hands
I wasn't there when you fell
I wasn't there when your blood
Rebellious as it can be
Refused to colour inside chalk lines
I wasn't there when you breathed your last

But I was here for the aftermath
I was here for the storm after the storm
For the trial of a dead man
I was here for your demonization
I was here for your canonization
I was here when we stole your name
Spoke it without your permission
Emblazoned it on our shirts
Etched it into our hats
Traded it in when it no longer fit our agenda
Or when the new models dropped into our timelines
I was here when we forgot you
Let your name fall off our lips
Replaced you with celebrity gossip

Made you just a Wikipedia article
A face in a funeral collage
Another dead thing.
Or rather

I was here when some refused to forget your name.
I was here when some decided to never forget you
To celebrate your life and mourn your death
To make you neither saint nor sinner
To make you human

To Tamir

I wanted to throw you a party
On your 13th birthday
I was gonna call it a Black Mitzvah
(That was clever right?)
And there would be food
A ceremony
A party
Lots of gifts
All celebrating you
Entering into manhood
I turned 13 once.
It was nice.
Everyone should have a 13th birthday.
It's pretty dope.
Being alive for it, I mean.
Being alive
For your 13th birthday.
That's cool, y'know...

[_____]

There is an empty space on a name tag
Hungry
Waiting for another name to devour
Ravenous
With teeth like knives
Hands like whips
Searching for another identity to consume
To chew and spit
To display and dispose
So many names
So many lives lost
So many lives shared
So many lives erased
Makes you weary
Makes you wonder just how quickly
Your name can be digested
Your name can be discarded
Will they say your name
Will they take your life
Condense its worth into argument
Declare your guilt
Proclaim your dead identity guilty or innocent
Discuss the worth in your skin
Call you ordinary dead thing
Write your name into this empty space
Only to erase your name
Your memory

To make way for the next

Skydive

And I fell
Weightless
For what seemed like a lifetime
Air, rushing past
The ground, a forlorn lover
Rushing to greet me
As one does when warriors return from battle

I am a child soldier
All man and anger and power and strength
All boy and fear and inability and weakness
Made manifest in the barrels of weapons held by
monsters
Made manifest in the eyes of those who call me
monster
Who call me beast
And hunt my skin for trophy

I am a child soldier
A fighter bred in concrete jungles
A lost childhood walking through war-torn
neighborhoods
Fallen into gutters of blood
Falling onto pyramid like street corners
Final post gunshot skydive
Parachute into the arms of God

Last Breath
In Case of Dying

This is it.
End of the brick road
Final countdown
Liftoff

I've made mistakes
Said some things to
people
Hurtful things
Terrible

But I think
I think that just maybe
I'm sorry
sorry

Sorry for lying
For making light of life
Of love
Sorry

All I ask
Now that I leave here
Singular request
Please

Remember my name
My life, my dreams, yes
Even mistakes
Failures

Keep me close
Though I add nothing
more
Love me
Still

And please know
That I loved, above all
My God
You

I'm leaving now
Waste no tears on me
But laugh
Smile

My eyes close
My voice sinks into soil
Remember me
Remember

The one where bullets are like a pharmaceutical drug

BLACKNESS

Symptoms:

Good rhythm
Well-seasoned chicken
Red Kool-Aid (made right every time)
Good music (see Good rhythm)
A hairstyle for every mood
Pride in heritage
Increased Melanin
Wallets
Skittles
Breathing
Swimming
Turning Signals
Praying

Cure:

9mm

Side effects:

Death

Semantic Satiation

Black lives matter.
Black lives matter.
Black lives matter.
Black lives matter.
Black lives matter.
Black lives matter.

Black lives matter.
Black ███████████
████ lives████
████ matter.
Black lives ████
████ lives matter.

_____ lives matter
_____ lives matter
_____ lives matter
_____ lives matter
_____ lives matter
_____ lives matter

Black lives matter.
Black boys matter.
Black girls matter.
Black Christians matter
Black Muslims matter
Black Atheists matter

Black men matter
Black women matter
Black poor matter
Black rich matter
Black young matter
Black elders matter

Black love matters
Black hurt matters
Black fear matters
Black rage matters
Black joy matters
Black pain matters

Black art matters
Black poetry matters
Black dance matters
Black theatre matters
Black music matters
Black film matters

Brown lives matter
Red lives matter
Yellow lives matters
Coloured lives matter
These lives matter
All lives matter, and

Black matters.
Black lives
Lives matter
Black.
Lives.
Matter.
Black lives matter.

[redacted]

When your bullets entered [redacted]'s body
Did you feel a mixture of [redacted] and [redacted]?
Did your hands [redacted] in the taking of another's
life
When you saw [redacted]'s body slump into the
ground
Blood pooling
Life waning
Did you play jury?
Declare him [redacted].
In your own trial
Will you stand tall
Stare into the eyes of a grieving [redacted]
Welling with tears
And declare yourself [redacted]?

Coloured

America, America, God shed His grace on thee
And crown thy good with brotherhood
from sea to shining sea.

And we are still drowning.
Trying to manufacture life rafts from rhetoric.
There is still the fear of swimming in my community.
There is still a fear of deep water
Like Amistad was documentary
Like Katrina was just another Monday.
Like pool parties are still dangerous in Dixie
There is a fear
Of blue water
And red blood
And the white at the end of the tunnel.
There is a fear
Of blue bloods
And red lights
And the whites of their skin
There is a fear of colour.
Of brown and black,
Of red and white and blue.

The one where bullets are like flowers

When a hollow point enters its target
It expands
Spreads out
Blossoming into its shape
Iron and lead, just like any other seed
Only needs a fertile place to plant itself
And it does.
By the hundreds
They are sown
And soon mature and grow
A macabre hibiscus
Blooming deep red
Unfurling wide their petals on the backs of walking
gardens
These seeds
Always prepared to break earth-like skin
Quenched with arterial waters
And yet still thirsty
Still yearning to create a bouquet in my skin
Looking for good soil
A nice, brown space
Filled with life
To feed itself from

This Time
(After Aurora)

iii.
I'm tired of singing this song
Of dancing this dance
Of making this piece my magnum opus.
You would think that I would have learned by now
That wallets be mistaken for grenades.
You would think that I would have learned by now
That stealing cigars is a crime
Punishable by firing squad.
You would think that I would have learned that to
some,
My blood is meant to flow and pool
And color sidewalks red see
Clearly we are meant to be macabre art exhibits.

This time it was a movie theatre in Colorado.
Where folks only sought the refuge of a comic book
universe
With no inkling of the Joker to be introduced into
their lives
And I wonder how Batman willingly allows the
villain to live and let innocents die.
And don't get me wrong.
I'm not saying that I wish the gunman died,

But in the wake of a massacre
Rifle toting super villain walks
Oxygen, stolen from his victims
Still parting his lips
But innocent men with moonlight skin
Are made to be shadow
Dark Knights
Fallen to the breath
Of fire breathing dragons

Genesis

In the beginning,
God was God
Ruler and master
Speaker of worlds
Name synonymous with eternity
And He saw fit
Needing nothing to complete his being
To create
And He did

And God said
Let us make man in our own image and likeness.
And He created them
Man and woman
Black and white
He created them
And God saw the black and said that it was good
And God saw the white and said that it was good

In the end
god was currency
god was rhetoric
god was death
god was an elementary school in Sandy Hook
god was a movie theatre in Aurora
god was a church in Charleston

god was every single monogrammed bullet that
flew into darkened bodies
god was an artist's portfolio of a bloodied canvas
god was the separation between colour

Eli, Eli, lema sabachthani?

Phobia

Some of us are afraid of heights.
Some are afraid of loud noises, enclosed spaces
and strangers.
Some are afraid of the dark and some are afraid of
white.
Some of us are afraid of monsters in closets
Boogeymen under beds
And spiders in our home.

Some are afraid of daddy coming home
Or daddy leaving again.
Some are afraid of mama.
Some are afraid for mama.
Some are afraid that mama knew best
And mama was right
And mama is gone
And mama, it's too late for me.

Some of us are afraid of being too late.
Some of us are afraid of leaving too early.
Some are afraid of others leaving
Like a great immigration
To the shores of another friendship.

Some are afraid of friendship, and of relationship,
Of laced fingers, of late night talks,
Of light kisses, and long walks.

Some are afraid of lump in throat
Filled with guilt and disappointment.
Some are afraid of disappointment or disappointing
Or disapproval or this heartbreak
Or decision or this time
Or disability or this face or disgrace.

Some of us are afraid of this grace that spurs
Limbs to dance and heart to sing.
Some are afraid to sing
And scratch raw the throats of those who are afraid
to stay silent.

Some are afraid of silence
Of the eye of the hurricane
Of the calm before the storm
Some of us are afraid of life imitating storm
Of life imitating movies
Of life imitating history
Of life imitating death.
Some are afraid of death
And heaven and hell
And ghosts and underworld.
Some are afraid of life imitating underworld.

Some of us are afraid of Satan and some of us are
afraid of God.
Some of us are afraid of meeting either too early.

Of feeling the sting of death
Of feeling the victory of grave

Some of us are afraid of feeling
Or not feeling
Or whatever lies in between that.
Some of us are afraid of fear
Some of us are afraid to fear.
Some of us are afraid that our fears for our future
are unfounded
That our trials transform minds into caged birds
who have forgotten their song.

Some of us are afraid of cages.
Some of us are afraid of chains and whips
And chain gangs and whiplashes.
Some of us are afraid of stereotypes and
judgments
And typecasting and profiling
And some of us are afraid of shapes that don't fit
inside our box.
Some are afraid of these things and have the
opportunity of picking and choosing what is scary to
them.

I am afraid of heights.
I am afraid of loud gunshots, enclosed coffins and
uniformed strangers.

I do not have the luxury to pick and choose my phobias.
I walk in nightmare calling for God to remind me He is near
To lend me His peace
To lend me His voice.
I am afraid of His silence.

Young Black Men

(After "Old Black Men" by Georgia Douglass Johnson)

I have dreamed, as young men dream
Of glory, riches, and fame.
Of days spent on beaches
Of getting caught unexpectedly in the rain.

I have hoped, indeed as youth hope
Of first job, first car, first house.
Of bended knee and broom jumping
Of candlelit dinners with spouse

I have seen, as many have seen
Lives transform into dust and smoke
Seen mothers mourn their setting sons
Seen my pain to be made into a joke

I have learned, as all must learn
Of grey hair and age
Learned of death's indiscriminate hand
Of the period at the end of the page

This Time

(After Micah)

iv.
I am tired of writing this poem
Of preaching this sermon.
I'm tired of explaining to my two youngest brothers
that they matter.
That their hopes and dreams are valid
And bright
And possible.
Micah wants to be a paleontologist.
He spends time photocopying an encyclopedia's
worth of information
About every dinosaur he can find into his memory,
Watches anything he can about the Jurassic era,
And he is SO fascinated by fossils.
I have to let him know that he is not meant to be a
fossil.
That he is not meant to be buried and remembered.
That he is not a valley of dry bones.
That he is not meant to be extinct.

Writer's Block

I'm trying to write a poem
About cupcakes and flowers
And unicorns gracefully leaping over rainbows
With glitter
You know, deep topics
But try as I might
I only use the ashes of dead bodies as lead
Spilled street corner blood as ink
Dead men's names as titles
I have made a career of being carefree
Cheshire smile
Living like I have the right
To the pursuit of happiness
But now, I pray
That I do not become
Prey
The trophy to those who would poach my skin

Working Title

(After Mahogany L. Browne)

The name of this poem is

I am not afraid, or

I am not a living epitaph, or

I am not a walking death knell, or

I am not an endangered species, or

I am not a chalk outline, or

I am not target practice, or

I am not murder statistic
theft statistic
rape statistic, or

I am not your nigger, or

I am not a monster, or

I am not a felony charge, or

I am not domestic terrorist, or
I am not stereotype, or

I am not my own elegy, or

I am not an early obituary, or

I am not grim reaper, or

I am not worthless, or

You are not worthless, or

We are not worthless, or

We are not worthless, or

We are not worthless

Iced Coffee

i.
Dear Lord
If you can hear me
There are things I do not tell you
Feelings that I hide in my heart
Forgetting that you live there too

ii.
I am writing this in a coffee shop.
Plain iced coffee
Two sugars
Half + half
Bright and sweet
A bit bitter
The taste of contrast
A treat on a hot summer's day

iii.
I have counted six black people
Beautiful people
Passing the window
On the UWS
We walk with our swagger
Our pride
Our honour
Our heritage
Etched into our very skin

Skin that fears being split open
That fears being forfeit
Fears being forsaken
Fears being forgotten

iv.
Dear Lord
If you are listening
There are things I do not tell you
Feelings I hide deep in my heart
I have never stopped trusting You
But I have stopped trusting your people
Your people, Cruel
Your people, Kill

v.
I am drinking iced coffee
Bright and sweet
Like the insides of my hands
Or the dreams of a young boy from Brooklyn
A bit bitter
Like an unwanted obituary
Or the trial of a ghost
Soon I will finish it
And have to leave this place
Leave this respite

vi.
Dear Lord
I have finished my iced coffee
My relief is over

I feel the heat again

A Night Prayer

Hear now, and answer me, O Lord
For your servant bears the weight of fear on his
back
Hear me, O Lord
For there are those who would seek to devour me
Those whose hands are animal traps
Whose mouths are ravenous wolves shirking their
lambs wool coats
Whose eyes are wildfires in drought

My God
I pray you protect us
I pray that when the night sky matches our skin
That when the suns in our eyes seek to set
That when our heads lower with the moon rise
That Your hand cover Your children
That the way of the innocent be safe
That You remain Lord over the just and the unjust

Human Nature

Do you think that Jesus got scared?
Did His divine heart ever skip a beat?
Did the Breather of life ever feel breathless?
In my yearning to be like my Lord, I wonder...
Did I ever have a nervous Saviour?
Did He mourn others as He did Lazarus?
Did He mourn others often?
Did Jesus ever mourn so often that He began to
think of his own impending death?
Looming like preconstructed crucifix?
Substitute innocent lives with his own?
Did Jesus ever walk past men
With Klan-like eyes
The same men He breathed life into
Knowing that they would be the death of Him?
Did he write His own eulogy?
Was there ever a moment
When my Saviour, Jesus the Christ
Had to remind himself that His life mattered?
That though His crown be thorns
Though His robe be bloodied
Though His verdict be guilty
Though His heart be innocent
Though His skin be darker
Though His image be lighter
Though His men kill Him
Deny Him

Renounce Him
Label Him criminal
Call him Monster
Ignore his surrender
Did He ever have to tell Himself
That His brown skin
That His curled hair
That His weathered feet and calloused hands
That these were valuable?
That He was still royalty?

Because sometimes
I do.

This Time
(The Last Time)

v.

I'm tired of writing this poem.

I'm tired of painting this picture.

I'm tired of carving this tombstone.

This time, it was a boy in a hoodie.

This time, it was an immigrant reaching for his wallet.

This time, it was an asthmatic who broke up a fight.

This time, it was a boy who whistled.

This time, it was a girl at a pool party.

This time, it was a woman with a broken taillight.

This time, it was an innocent Rabbi unjustly executed

This time always seems to be more shocking than last time.

This time, maybe our voices will be heard.

This time, maybe I won't craft headstones out of hashtags.

This time, maybe our words won't origami themselves into obituaries.

This time, maybe we will matter.

It just frightens me that there probably will be a next time.

Afterword

I can't say that this book is a dream come true, because four years ago, when I began writing, I would never have even dreamed of writing an entire book's worth of poetry. And here we are now. What you have in your hands are the musings of an opera singer with too much time on his hands, a teacher writing down thoughts during his commute, a Christian bored in the middle of Sunday service, a black man struggling to not fit the profile and a young adult scared out of his mind for what the future holds.

But along with that, what you have here is a miracle. I will be the first to tell you that there are better writers than me in the world. There are those who have been writing since before I was born, and there will be those whose library of works will far outpace my own. I have friends whose prowess with the pen as well as the stage completely astound me, and I can't help but to envy the gifts that God has given them. But still, I felt the push from colleagues and family alike to work on and release this project.

This is by no means a perfect book. There may be things in here that you don't like. There will be ideas that you want fleshed out a bit more, or concepts that you want a little less of, but that is beside the point. This book's purpose is to uplift, educate, inspire, and start a dialogue. If after reading a poem, you feel any of those feelings, then I have done what I feel is my job as a poet.

So there it is. In your hands, you either have the one that started it all, or my one shot attempt in creating something meaningful. The thing is, even if this is the pinnacle of my poetry career, even if I never write another word of prose, this is still more than I ever thought I was capable of. And for sharing this time with me, I thank you. You are a part of something that shouldn't have happened, but it did, by the grace of God.

God Bless

C. Lilley

About the Author

C. Lilley (born Christopher Lilley) is a classically trained vocalist and multi-instrumentalist. He brings warmth and vulnerability to a soul and folk filled sound. C uses his gift on multiple instruments to craft stories filled with transparency and honesty. Floating between the sounds of gospel and soul and the likes of acoustic folk and blues, C uses his love for people and his love for God to build dialogue around mental health, masculinity, and life after.

From the start of his artistic journey as a spoken word poet, C has had the privilege of performing with the likes of Jasmine Mans and Prentiss Powell, and has performed in several famed spaces such as the Nuyorican Poets Cafe and the Bowery Poetry Club, as well as in venues across the country. He also had the privilege of being on the Brooklyn Slam Team which placed 2nd in the National Poetry Slam in Denver, Colorado.

Finally stretching his musical legs, C is seeking to break down the walls of toxic masculinity, racism, spiritual abuse, and mental health stigma one song or poem at a time. #BreakStigmasTogether

C is the author of The Quiet Way, and je suis noir [i am black], available now at clilleyartist.com.

www.ingramcontent.com/pod-product-compliance
Lightning Source LLC
Chambersburg PA
CBHW032057040426
42449CB00007B/1108